LIVING IN THE SUNLIGHT
MAKING A FORGOTTEN MEDITATION AN ATOMIC HABIT

STEVE KING

IN PERPETUITY PUBLISHING
Canberra

Copyright © 2022 Steve King and Ordo Templi Orientis (Australia)

Writings of Aleister Crowley © 2022 Ordo Templi Orientis (International)

All rights reserved. This book and any portion thereof may not be reproduced or used in any manner whatsoever without the express written permission of the publisher (other than for review purposes).

First Printing 2022
ISBN 978-0-6451039-4-6
Ordo Templi Orientis
GPO Box 1193
Canberra, ACT 2601
Australia

www.otoaustralia.org.au
livinginthesunlight.site

In Perpetuity Publishing is an imprint of Ordo Templi Orientis (Australia)

Cover and internal design by **honeyrogue.com**

CONTENTS

Introduction

1. Getting started

2. Abodes of Night

3. Abodes of Morning

4. Abodes of Day

5. Abodes of Evening

6. The Starry Abode

7. The Stainless Abode

8. Living in the Sunlight

Appendix
Stepping Out of the Old Aeon and Into the New

Works Cited

The day *is* thine,
the night also *is* thine:
thou hast prepared
the light and the sun.
Psalm 74:16

Introduction

Even as a man ascending a steep mountain is lost to the sight of his friends in the valley, so must the adept seem. They shall say: He is lost in the clouds. But he shall rejoice in the sunlight above them, and come to the eternal snows.
— *Liber X*:15

Living in the Sunlight is a practice that entered the tradition of *Thelema* and the religious Order OTO (Ordo Templi Orientis) - the Order of Oriental Templars, or Order of the Temple of the East. It is a simple exercise that needn't take more than a few minutes daily and which anyone can do. You don't need to be a *Thelemite* (someone who accepts the Law of Thelema) or be an initiate of the OTO. There are no special requirements or conditions, physical or spiritual. Nor is any prior knowledge or experience needed.

Living in the Sunlight is a *practice of self awareness for vitality*. It uses the restorative power of sleep and the regenerative power of the Sun, coupled with the firm *intention* to let go of the harmful and hurtful. You identify with the Sun instead, the source of Life on earth, drawing forth its energies with a *heliocentric* mindset. It is like an active meditation or a *prayer*. You will literally *become the Sun*.

The practice and benefits of Living in the Sunlight are cumulative and amass over time. A good analogy might be how a regular *vipassana* practice (even its secular *mindfulness* variety) can have a gradual and seemingly automatic effect on your wellbeing. You may not be able to pinpoint exactly how or when it happened, but you realise you've changed and are changing for the better; perhaps you're more present, or aware, or calm. The same applies here.

This idea of a regular practice that leads to breakthrough moments is important. These critical thresholds in Living in the Sunlight unlock new levels of glow, flow and insight. You'll bring joy to yourself and to those around you. Living in the Sunlight works best as what James Clear called an *atomic habit* - a practice or habit whose power lies in the aggregation of marginal gains, and the neuroscience and behavioural psychology behind that. Not just any old habit mind you, but a little habit that is part of a larger system. *There is no larger system than the solar.*

This book is about aligning, receiving and revivifying your Being in this system. "Just as atoms are the building blocks of molecules, *atomic habits* are the building blocks of remarkable results ... This is the meaning of the phrase atomic habits - a regular practice or routine that is not only small and easy to do, but also the source of incredible power." Power radiates, reflects and relates - that's why Living in the Sunlight is as much for the sentient beings around you as it is for yourself. As Clear states, "Relationships compound. People reflect your behavior back to you."

While the Living in the Sunlight practice can be described in a few sentences (and it will be), this short primer gives you its background and context. The extra detail may be of particular benefit to those of you whose analytical minds find it hard to suspend disbelief. It can also help to position your practice as a contemplative, psychophysical exercise, beyond simple affirmation.

I should stress that there is nothing particularly radical or revolutionary about Living in the Sunlight. It is not a long lost secret or some new hack to the superhuman. It is simply a way to *let go or surrender to the present moment*. In this regard it is comparable to contemplative prescriptions found in many cultures, some thousands of years old. Where Living in the Sunlight differs is that while you banish or let go of the injurious, you actively invoke or identify with the integrous, irradiating the 'sunlight' within while radiating without. You'll be kinder to yourself and others, centered and joyous amidst the fluctuating days, nights and seasons of life's vicissitudes.

Living in the Sunlight has been mostly overlooked for the 100 or so years since its adoption by the founder of Thelema, British magus and former head of OTO, Aleister Crowley (1875-1947). Perhaps it was not given much attention or taken too seriously due to its very simplicity, combined with a certain amount of historical obfuscation. In any event, it has gone mostly unnoticed in the archives of the Order.

Up until now.

How to use this book

The Living in the Sunlight practice is given in Chapters 6 and 7. It may be tempting to jump straight to there or to skim over the preceding material, but I advise against it. The early Chapters provide the foundational framework, background, context, and concepts that need to be integrated in order to make the practice come alive. These should be reflected on and returned to as you develop the habit of practice.

This short book is my humble contribution to the people of the world who might find it, in these times of pandemic disruption. It is one small way towards recalibrating and centering during this period of the new normal, change, uncertainty and recovery.

I wish to thank the In Perpetuity Press team for encouraging me to put down on paper for all what I had been teaching one to one for a few.

I am grateful to Hymenaeus Beta, Frater Superior and Outer Head of the OTO, who shared with me the source letter 25 years ago. I have been experimenting and practicing ever since.

Chapter 1
Getting started

What actually goes on when we meditate? How can this be explained as simply and straightforwardly as possible?

In any meditation practice, we are working with and experiencing the Mind, Body and Spirit. Taken together, this conceptual framework is vague and overused, often not skilfully. Let me try and clear that up.

Consider first of all your Body. It might seem a little strange to think about, but your Body cannot actually experience itself. An arm has no experience of its 'arminess' nor a body its 'bodyness.' They cannot experience their position in space or their own bodily sensations. *Body has to be experienced in the Mind.*

The Mind has no experience of itself either. Your thoughts, feelings, and memories cannot experience themselves.
They are experienced via the Mind in something greater than Mind, that we call Spirit. Another name for Spirit as used here is Consciousness. *Mind has to be experienced in Consciousness.*

Consciousness is limitless. It has no dimension or form. Your 'bit' of it, the contents of your Consciousness - your experience of Consciousness - we call Awareness. *Consciousness has to be experienced in Awareness.*

From our Awareness is a knowingness of what is going on in Consciousness. Consciousness can then report on what is going on in Mind, and Mind can report on what is going on in Body.

That of which you are unaware, is Unconscious.

Ultimately *everything* goes on within the field of Consciousness. Any change to our experience of existence has to take place in Consciousness, through our Awareness. Importantly, by expanding our Awareness we can make the Unconscious conscious, thereby becoming more integrous, balanced and whole.

Awareness can be likened to Light, or a high frequency of *vibration*, within the *energy* field of Consciousness. You may not have thought of Consciousness as energy before, but we intuitively know when we are around people with positive energy (good vibes) or negative energy (bad vibes). If you consider different levels of Consciousness (eg. hatred, desire, pride, acceptance, reason, peace, etc.) and especially those levels you've directly experienced or have a tendency towards, the effects of their different energy levels on you are self-evident.

Now energy cannot be destroyed, only transformed. Ideally, we should be transforming in a *life affirming* way from negative to positive levels of energy or Consciousness. That takes Awareness, and where the attention of Awareness goes, energy will flow in that direction. *Living in the Sunlight is about getting this flow happening.*

Another name for this positive flow of energy is what the Swiss psychologist Carl Jung called the *inner drive of the Unconscious towards Wholeness*. He called Wholeness the transcendent principle or transpersonal Self, the self-ordering principle beyond Ego and duality. Jung even referred to the Self as the inner empirical deity or the God within. The God without is the Sun. In Jung's *Psychology of the Unconscious* he refers to the Sun as the fructifier and creator of all that lives, the source of energy in our world. "Our life substance, as an energic process is entirely Sun."

Jung uses the uncommon word *energic*. This is *not* a typo and it does *not* mean energetic. It means a spiritual or ethereal energy held to be present in all living things. We are all of the Sun. Jung further identified the Sun with "that driving strength of our own soul, which we call libido, and whose nature it is to allow the useful and injurious, the good and bad to proceed." To what end? For the drive to Wholeness. Jung you could say was Living in the Libido! Same difference.

This simplified Mind, Body and Spirit framework *basically* describes the process of Consciousness in many of the world's mystical and magical systems. I say 'basically' as it can be taken to more detailed and granular levels of introspection and experience in the Mystery Schools. Obviously, when considering *any* map of Consciousness, you could always lock horns or split hairs on detail and definition. But they are all variations upon the one Mind, Body, Spirit theme, differing only in specialization, emphasis or modality.

If you are Living in the Sunlight your interior condition will be aligned towards positivity and Wholeness, free of self-limiting mental models and emotional domains. *For in the ever present Light of the Sun you are eternal, subject only to what you hold in Mind.* It was the Austrian-British philosopher Ludwig Wittgenstein who said that eternal life belongs to those who live in the present. And for Erwin Schrödinger, the cofounder of quantum physics, the present is the only thing that has no end.

Chapter 2
Abodes of Night

Living in the Sunlight is first mentioned in a letter from Aleister Crowley to his student Charles Stansfeld Jones (1886-1950). From the astrological details Crowley used to date the letter, we know it was written on 29 October 1915.

Our first step will be to take a good look at this mention and unpack it. This will first of all involve covering, condensing and contextualizing some background history. This will give you an overview of the people, circumstances and environment that enabled Living in the Sunlight.

Crowley makes two references in the letter to Living in the Sunlight.

Reference One:

"I must tell you more, too, about 'living in the sunlight,' which is our beloved Sister Hilarion's way of saying 'the way of the Tao.' I had hoped she would speak of it the other night, but she was shy. She taught it to me, and from that my whole life has been transfigured. In material matters, even, all has suddenly gone well. It is difficult to explain; I will ask her to write to you about it. The main point seems to be the conception of yourself as a King - Vide Liber CCXX Cap II. It's damnably hard to explain, but it's merely a trick, like all great skill, perfectly easy once you find the way. The elements of struggle, worry, desire, must be eliminated."

Reference Two:

"P.S. About this 'living in the sunlight,' I ought to add that it involves making everybody in your sphere reflect your radiance. This is the measure of your success. If you have anybody about you miserable, it shows that your light is failing to penetrate. This primarily applies to the private life, and to the Lodge, but also to casual strangers. And remember if you can do this, you can get away with robbery and murder! They won't care how strict you are; they'll all obey cheerfully without knowing that they are doing it. It will all be part of a glorious romp through life. I've not been a very striking success in the past, but in the last few months I've had a great teacher - not only precept, but example."

The first thing to mention, stating the obvious, is that the Living in the Sunlight letter is from the British magus Aleister Crowley. I won't dwell that much on Crowley in this book. If you want to know more about him, there are now quite a number of serious and scholarly biographies available. Seeing Crowley was in North America when he wrote this letter, Tobias Churton's *Aleister Crowley in America* is one relevant example.

It is possible or even probable that some readers are dismissive, fearful or even straight out anti-Crowley. Such is to be expected given his notorious public image and all of the sensationalist and fake news that he has been subject of. This book is not intended as an apologia. However, if you're a reader who falls into these categories, and with the last Chapter firmly in mind, you might want to ask yourself what is the level of consciousness and quality of energy being generated by your reaction to Crowley? What do you get in return? What is the Ego pay-off?

Let's take a slight detour and look into this some more.
It will probably come up in your own Living in the Sunlight
practice at some time or other over other persons or matters.
Behind thoughts are feelings. Suppressed and repressed
feelings accumulate pressure. Pressure persists as *resistance*
that keeps emotional pay-off feelings going. It is resistance
that creates and projects a 'demon Crowley' *out there* upon
which to vent or react. If it wasn't Crowley, it would be someone
or something else. *Meditation means to let go or surrender
all of that to the present moment.* It is a very particular way
of experiencing the world. Don't deny or resist. Dispassionately
observe and let feelings be and they will dissipate. They will
go. If you are inclined to bin this book over Crowley, the irony
is that Living in the Sunlight is exactly what you need! To live
in the sunlight is to take responsibility for your own shit.
No dumping it on others. Ever.

The next point to make is that this is an OTO letter. Crowley
signs it off using his official name as head of the English-
speaking OTO, "Baphomet" (the name of the idol reputedly
worshiped by the Knights Templar). The recipient of the Living
in the Sunlight letter, Charles Stansfeld Jones, is addressed
as "Very Illustrious Sir Knight and very dear Brother." That
is the address given in formal OTO correspondence to a VII°
(Seventh degree) initiate of the Order. And the letter is titled
"Given from the Sanctuary of the Gnosis." That means it
has come from Authority, the "Sanctuary of the Gnosis" of the
IX° (Ninth degree) of OTO being the custodians of the Order's
central and supreme gnosis, or secret knowledge. In other
words, Crowley is saying "pay close attention, this is important!"
His Machiavellian reference that Jones uses Living in the
Sunlight to control his OTO lodge needn't be read sinisterly
(or taken too seriously). It does exaggerate the premise that
irradiating within radiates without.

It is an open secret that OTO 'secret knowledge' pertains to a sexual doctrine, mysticism and magic. In fact, our letter here was part of a series of personal instructions Crowley had been giving Jones on its VII° level of application. Living in the Sunlight is mentioned in the course of this instruction as a *complementary practice*. While these matters pertain to the OTO, what I'm doing here is treating Living in the Sunlight as a standalone practice in its own right, suitable for anyone. There is nothing secret about it. That it appears in a letter otherwise dedicated to secret OTO mysteries highlights its value. There is obviously *a link between Living in the Sunlight and the doctrinal practices of OTO*. They are all working with that "life substance" Jung described as an "energic process" and "entirely Sun" in the previous Chapter.

Note as well from Reference One above that Living in the Sunlight was not something Crowley learned from OTO. It was taught to him by someone he names as his "beloved Sister Hilarion." It was this particular person's own unique method. She came up with it. She taught it to Crowley. He adopted it and taught it to Jones, in his OTO capacity. *This was always a personal practice before Crowley introduced it to OTO.*

So who was this beloved Sister Hilarion? Her name was Jeanne Robert Foster (1879-1970), an American fashion model, poet, editor, art and literary critic, and rumored 'secret correspondent' (or spy). Something of an all-round superwoman, Foster was friendly with John Butler Yeats, Ezra Pound and T.S. Elliot, among many others in literary, artistic and high society circles. She was also a Theosophist, deeply spiritually driven, and known throughout her life for her compassionate and considerate nature. Foster didn't shy away from asking the big questions and looking into her interior condition. For a while, Crowley and her were an item.

Although it was a hectic love triangle (or triangles), Foster and Crowley were lovers for about a year from mid-1915 to mid-1916. Foster participated in numerous sex magical operations with Crowley, adopting the magical name Hilarion from Theosophical Society lore. When Crowley wrote the Living in the Sunlight letter, the pair were at the height of their passion. Crowley's unpublished book of verse, *The Golden Rose*, is devoted exclusively to his love for Hilarion. The poems abound in solar-alchemical imagery and the sex magical Rose Cross symbolism of the OTO, Crowley the "White Lion of the Sun" and Hilarion the "Red Eagle of the Moon." It is some of Crowley's finest poetry - inspired and in love.

Some years after the relationship with Foster had ended, Crowley would still question in his diary, "Did she really break my heart?" He wrote that of no other. At that time life was not so radiant for Crowley. Hilarion had long gone. And the Living in the Sunlight practice had long disappeared.

Chapter 3
Abodes of Morning

With enough of the background to proceed, we can now look more closely at Crowley's references to Living in the Sunlight. First of all, Crowley describes Living in the Sunlight as "Hilarion's way of saying 'the way of the Tao.'"

I imagine that most readers have at least some familiarity with the Tao, a philosophy and religion from ancient China that emphasized harmony with the universe, with Tao - the source, pattern and substance of everything that exists. Most of us have probably heard of the interplay of the Yin and the Yang, of the union and harmony of opposites, of 'going with the flow'. This is Tao, the Way.

What precisely did Crowley mean by Tao in 1915? I cannot stress enough that during the World War One years in North America, Crowley immersed himself in the Tao. It is a lengthy topic that has been mostly overlooked or underrated by Western researchers (and students) of Crowley. To give you some idea of Crowley's engagement with Taoism at this time, within a few years of the Living in the Sunlight letter, Crowley produced new translations of the Taoist classics, the *Tao Te Ching* and the *Ch'ing-ching Ching*. He also recalled his previous incarnation as the Taoist philosopher and alchemist, Ko Hsüan (Ge Xuan), the author of the *Ch'ing-ching Ching* ("The Classic of Purity").

Crowley was assisted in his Taoist projects by a discarnate adept he referred to as the Wizard Amalantrah. If you need to suspend disbelief in order to entertain discarnate wizards, go right ahead. Another way to look at it is that consistent with the tradition of Taoist mysticism, Crowley the mystic had encountered a Taoist Immortal. Crowley's Taoist works must be judged on their own merit. "The proof of the pudding is in the eating."

Around the same time as his dealings with the Wizard, Crowley penned one of his finest and most inspired epistles, *Liber Aleph*. It was written for Charles Stansfeld Jones, the student he wrote the Living in the Sunlight letter to. The Tao is mentioned in 12 of the book's 208 analects, although the epistle as a whole reads like a sublime Taoist treatise. As it is basically contemporaneous with the Living in the Sunlight letter, we will look to answer our question there.

In *Liber Aleph*, Crowley describes the Way of the Tao as the "Doctrine of doing everything by doing nothing" (Analect 29), it is that "which achieveth all Things by doing nothing" (Analect 57) and "the true Nature of Things, being itself a Way or Going, that is, a kinetic and not a static Conception" (Analect 69). Living in the Sunlight can therefore be considered the Way of doing everything by doing nothing, the Way of achieving all things and the true Nature of Things.

Paradoxically, "doing nothing" is kinetic - it relates or results from motion. Whatever this motion might be, Crowley makes a point of saying (twice) that it is hard to explain, which isn't terribly helpful. However, he gives us a clue when he stipulates "The elements of struggle, worry, desire, must be eliminated." Recalling the Introduction and Chapter 1, these are all at the negative end of the spectrum of the energy levels of Consciousness: "Ideally, we should be transforming in a life affirming way from negative to positive levels of energy or Consciousness. That takes Awareness, and where the attention of Awareness goes, energy will flow in that direction. *Living in the Sunlight is about getting this flow happening.*" That flow is the motion.

Keep in mind that when I describe these energies lineally and directionally (ie. opposite ends of a spectrum, negative to positive), this is both a convenience and limitation of language. The negatives are basically those lower Consciousness levels where the Ego dominates, based primarily on animal survival (pleasure, predation, gain). The positives demarcate a shift from that (animal) *force* to (spiritual) *power*, typified by a transformative energy resulting in the progressive awareness of Truth.

Another word for that transformative energy is Love, which initially presents itself in any move from the negative to a life affirming flow in the *Courage to change*. "Courage is the beginning of virtue" (*Liber XXX*). Love is union, in ultimate terms that inward drive (motion) to Wholeness or Self, which is also dissolution of the egoic 'self.' It presents in the willingness to try new things and accept personal responsibility and accountability. It animates the spiritual and spiritualizes the animal. Summoning up Courage requires the willingness to look at the *feeling* underlying a negative habit, reaction or mood (eg. in Crowley's letter; struggle, worry, desire) and through that Awareness begin to surrender it (or in Crowley's language, eliminate it). I mentioned this in relation to the 'demon Crowley' earlier. The more you can let go, the more Courage and self-esteem you can muster. In our particular case we do so to set in *motion* Living in the Sunlight.

Given the simplicity of the Sunlight practice, to summon enough Courage (to eliminate enough negativity) is relatively easy. It will build with consistency and repetition, which helps with the more deep seated or prolonged tendencies you might need to work on. Practice makes perfect, but as you will see, to commence is easy. Remember what Crowley said: Living in the Sunlight is "merely a trick, like all great skill, perfectly easy once you find the way."

Chapter 4
Abodes of Day

Crowley also tried to summarize the Tao of Living in the Sunlight as "The main point seems to be the conception of yourself as a King - Vide Liber CCXX Cap II." For those not familiar with Crowley's works this will take some explaining.

"Vide Liber CCXX Cap II" means consult Book 220 Chapter 2. This is *The Book of the Law* or *Liber AL vel Legis*, the revelatory text Crowley received by direct voice dictation from a praeterhuman intelligence in Cairo, Egypt, in 1904. Of all of the revealed or sacred writings of Thelema, this one is first and foremost. It was numbered 220 in Crowley's system of classifying the Thelemic canon.

The Book of the Law announced a new age or Aeon for humanity, a transition from the religions and worldviews of the Dying God era (eg. Osiris, Jesus) to a new age of the Crowned and Conquering Child (Horus). It was a shift from the Patriarchal Aeon of the Father to a new and futurist, emerging Aeon of the Child. The old world's systems and paradigms were either abrogated or to be reimagined and superseded by a radical and revolutionary influx of new ideas, approaches, knowledge, technology, worship, ethics, morality and understanding of the human condition. As this New Aeon unfolds, things would change at a rapid and disruptive pace. For Crowley and those who accept the Law of Thelema, *The Book of the Law* conceals and reveals the practical and esoteric Keys to this.

A Jungian perspective might be that in the early 20th century the old archetypal dominants had fallen into decay and were being replaced by new ones taking shape (signified by the avenging child god Horus as the evolved and evolving *Imago Dei*). This is no light subject and those interested should consult Crowley biographies or source texts. For a psychological reading and contextualization of Thelema, I highly recommend *Initiation in the Aeon of the Child* and *The Angel & the Abyss* by J. Daniel Gunther.

To make this reference by Crowley to *The Book of the Law* even more opaque, its official and inspired Comment included the instruction, "All questions of the Law are to be decided only by appeal to my writings, each for himself." An ordinary reading of this suggests that each individual must decide upon the book's meanings for themself. That includes "the conception of yourself as a King."

So far as our letter goes however, bear in mind that Crowley was writing to one of his closest students and confidantes at that time. It is likely that Jones had been privately instructed and shared a mutual understanding with Crowley on what the concept of a King meant. In the letter to Jones, Crowley was writing in shorthand so to speak, to somebody in the know. We do not know what that meaning was, but based upon the particular approach adopted in this book, there is a way by which we can approach it.

In Chapter 2 of *The Book of the Law* there are 15 references to Kings (singular and plural, capitalized and not). Crowley's popular Commentary to the book, *The Law is for All*, can be both instructive and suggestive for those who would pursue such a study. At times the Commentary needs to be read with your feet firmly planted on the ground, putting into context Crowley's banter and bravado amidst inspired insights, visionary forecasts and learned doctrine. Importantly, Crowley notes that in the book's conception of Kings, they cannot die or be hurt. He also says "'The Kings' are evidently those men who are capable of understanding Themselves." Living in the Sunlight opens up that capability (to *all* gender identities) in a deeply reflexive and reflective manner. As quoted in Chapter 1, "eternal life belongs to those who live in the present" - these are the Kings who cannot die or be hurt - and "the present is the only thing that has no end."

In a commentary to one of the other holy books of Thelema, Crowley noted that a King represents *the authority by which we rule our lives*. Adopting this meaning, we can add to our conception of a King above and treat Living in the Sunlight as a rule of life. This rule has to be both "the true nature of Things" and "Perfectly easy once you find the way." Now the authority is the Sun, material and spiritual. We rule our lives by it. We identify with (become Aware of) the energic solar light, the sunlight of earlier Chapters. In Jungian terms, it is to function from "that driving strength of our own soul, which we call libido" rather than be located in (and reacting to) "the useful and injurious, the good and bad" which it allows to proceed in the drive to Wholeness. The Kings are those capable of understanding this, their true selves. It is a gradual and perhaps fluctuating transition from the animal to the spiritual, from the energetic to the energic, from the Ego to the Solar (Self) point of view. You are shifting the seat of Consciousness to a new experience of reality.

When describing the effect of the practice in the letter to Jones, Crowley uses an unusual word that illustrates this. He says that after commencing Living in the Sunlight, "my whole life has been *transfigured*." (Italics mine). The word 'transfigure' is rare and more often than not used as a not quite correct synonym for the more common word, *transform*. In our 21st Century world for example, the modern workplace might undergo a 'digital transformation,' not a 'digital transfiguration.' And a gym goer might sign up for a 'body transformation,' not a 'body transfiguration.'

Why did Crowley, a master of the English language, choose one word over the other?

Transform means "a marked change in appearance or character, especially one for the better," while transfigure means "a large change in appearance or form." One is *marked*, the other *large*. Transfigure also means a "metamorphosis." So, beyond a large change it is also an "*abrupt* developmental change." In the Living in the Sunlight letter Crowley stresses, for example, "all has *suddenly* gone well." (emphasis mine). These sudden and abrupt changes are those threshold moments in atomic habits referred to in the Introduction. Transfigure can also mean, complementary to a large and abrupt change, a change that "glorifies and exalts." To rule our lives with authority (Kings), we are to *developmentally* change to a glorious and exalted state. We are therefore talking about a change far more impactful than just a "marked" and "for the better" transformation.

What we know so far then, is that by having the Courage to face and overcome the negative energies or Consciousness levels (Crowley for example cites struggle, worry, and desire), we can bring about large and abrupt *developmental* change which exalts and glorifies us. The trick to do this is the Way of the Tao. That trick is to set in motion a flow (kinesis) towards the life-affirming levels of Consciousness. And this naturally and (more or less) effortlessly happens or goes with the flow, the universal harmony of Tao.

Bear in mind, the Courage I first mentioned in Chapter 3, the beginning of Virtue, is a portal, not an end in itself. It is a gateway to higher outcomes. By refusing to resist the negative feelings, we overcome or eliminate them naturally, reaching those more *exalted* levels such as Acceptance or similar, and these in turn bring us into the *glorified* inner states such as Calm and Joy. Things run off their own motion or volition. It's as if we did nothing but set the ball rolling

Living in the Sunlight is a small and incremental practice that can lead to this surrender to Sun-Self, Jung's fructifier and creator of all that lives and "that driving strength of our own soul." Baphomet represents their macrocosmic and microcosmic reconciliation and Unity. It is a formula of Love.

In Chapter 67 of the *Tao Te Ching*, the Taoist "three treasures" are referred to as Compassion, Austerity and Reluctance (to excel). Noting my earlier remark that true Courage is Compassion, a phrase from Chapter 67 in the Red Pine translation reads "because I'm compassionate I can be valiant." That is to conceive of yourself as a King. As distinct from passivity due to emotional responses that cause inhibition, Compassion is the basis for effective and decisive action. Crowley translated what he called the "three jewels" as Gentleness (Compassion), Economy (Austerity) and Humility (Reluctance). In his *Tao Te Ching* he wrote (Chapter 67):

"That gentleness maketh me courageous, that economy generous, that humility honored. Men of today abandon gentleness for violence, economy for extravagance, humility for pride: this is death. Gentleness bringeth victory in fight; and holdeth its ground with assurance. Heaven wardeth the gentle man, by that same virtue."

Living in the Sunlight is one very simple (and gentle) way of undoing our programmed and reactive structures of maladaptive feeling and behaviors. The pervasiveness of guilt in modern society, for example, projected by the common mind onto the world around it, is a product and program of the morals and dogma of a superseded *Imago Dei*. The Sun has been clouded for centuries, hidden by the edifices of blind faith, original sin and their dark shadows. This has led to psychological and emotional corruption, self-destruction, decay, dispersion, denial and escapism.

The great discovery of psychology, the Ego, while a biological inheritance, is by nature fearful and limited. The animal life from which humans evolved depended upon the acquisition of energy from external sources, from the environment, and that principle remains at the core of the Ego (self-interest, rivalry etc), while no less engendering curiosity and our capacity for learning. Our evolutionary journey's survival mechanism then elaborated into intelligence, and the capacity from experience to acquire, process and integrate information in increasingly complex stratifications. This quality to the energy of life is innate.

While the psychologist is content to use these latter capacities to train the Ego to be 'acceptable' and 'well-adjusted,' by going beyond set limitations to more complex stratifications, by aligning to higher levels (vibrations) of Consciousness (energy) in day to day life, we achieve inner well-being, inner freedom, vital energy and energized enthusiasm.
The innocent child or True Self comes forth crowned (King) and conquering (Compassion). Major changes in life (changes in perception) can happen from seemingly small, random or trivial overcomings. This is a result of the Ego being a series of interlocking yet incoherent building blocks. Shifting one shifts the others. By adjusting our basic attitude, we attract - we increase our Awareness of - the entirety of the field of Consciousness (we make the Unconscious conscious). This alters the personality and benefits both ourselves and others. That Way of Compassion is Living in the Sunlight. We prelude that merging in the Universal (or Phallic) Consciousness that is the Way of the Yogi, Mystic or Initiate.

This is vividly expressed in *Liber CDXVIII The Vision and the Voice*, the Apocalypse of Thelema:

"This wine is such that its virtue radiateth through the cup, and I reel under the intoxication of it. And every thought is destroyed by it. It abideth alone, and its name is Compassion. I understand by "Compassion," the sacrament of suffering, partaken of by the true worshippers of the Highest. And it is an ecstasy in which there is no trace of pain. Its passivity (= passion) is like the giving up of the self to the beloved."

This Chapter may have been a lot to get your head around, and it might seem like I introduced Compassion as a convenience to fit in with the Baphomet (and OTO) thesis. I can only stress that as we move towards the spiritual and life affirming energies, beginning with Courage, on the inner drive to Wholeness, Compassion is psychological law. Another portal along the Way.

While I was looking over the draft to this Chapter one of those fortuitous synchronicities occurred when a friend and Brother, Joel Brady from Canberra, unexpectedly sent me the latest draft of his detailed study of Baphomet, for comment. Joel is researching the Baphomet motif across religious iconography, exploring it as an archetype and state of Consciousness.

Interestingly, Joel identifies this Consciousness with a closely associated religious term of relevance here, *kingly power*. Exploring this from Ancient Egypt, to the theology of the Temple surrounding the Holy of Holies, to the religious milieu of the Near and Middle East, and even in more recent expressions, one of many relevant examples he identifies is in Wagner's account of the Grail legend:

"Parsifal as the Bodhisattva awakens (from the life-dream) to Buddhahood and becomes a fountain of karma (merit). Then instead of entering into nirvana he chooses to pause on the threshold out of his great compassion (Sanskrit: mahākaruṇā) for those sentient beings who are still trapped in samsara, the cycle of rebirth, suffering and death." *The same can be said of the Compassion of Self to Ego and the inward drive to Wholeness.*

Earlier I had mentioned "the positives [levels of energy/Consciousness] demarcate a shift from that (animal) *force* to (spiritual) *power."* That shift is not a rejection per se, but rather a compassionate and enlightened reconciliation and raising. Transfiguration. Baphomet is a formula of love.

Interestingly, Joel arrived at similar conclusions to this Chapter: "All this interacts with the teachings of the admirable Soror Hilarion, as interpreted by Crowley, regarding the practice uncovered and explored by Frater Shiva X°[OTO] called "Living in the Sunlight", and the "Kingly Power"... This seems very close to the concept above of the IX° [OTO] who 'illumine them that sit in darkness and the shadow of death'. The IX° radiates the light from themselves, from the Sovereign Sanctuary, for the benefit of the brethren, and this is the way of the Tao."

It puts an interesting new twist on an old hymn:

"By your kingly power, O risen Lord, All that Adam lost is now restored: In your resurrection be adored."

Aleister Crowley in full OTO regalia about the time of Living in the Sunlight. Portrait by Arnold Genthe, originally published in The Equinox III:1 (1919)

Jeanne Robert Foster about the time of Living in the Sunlight, pencil on buff paper by John Butler Yeats (1917)

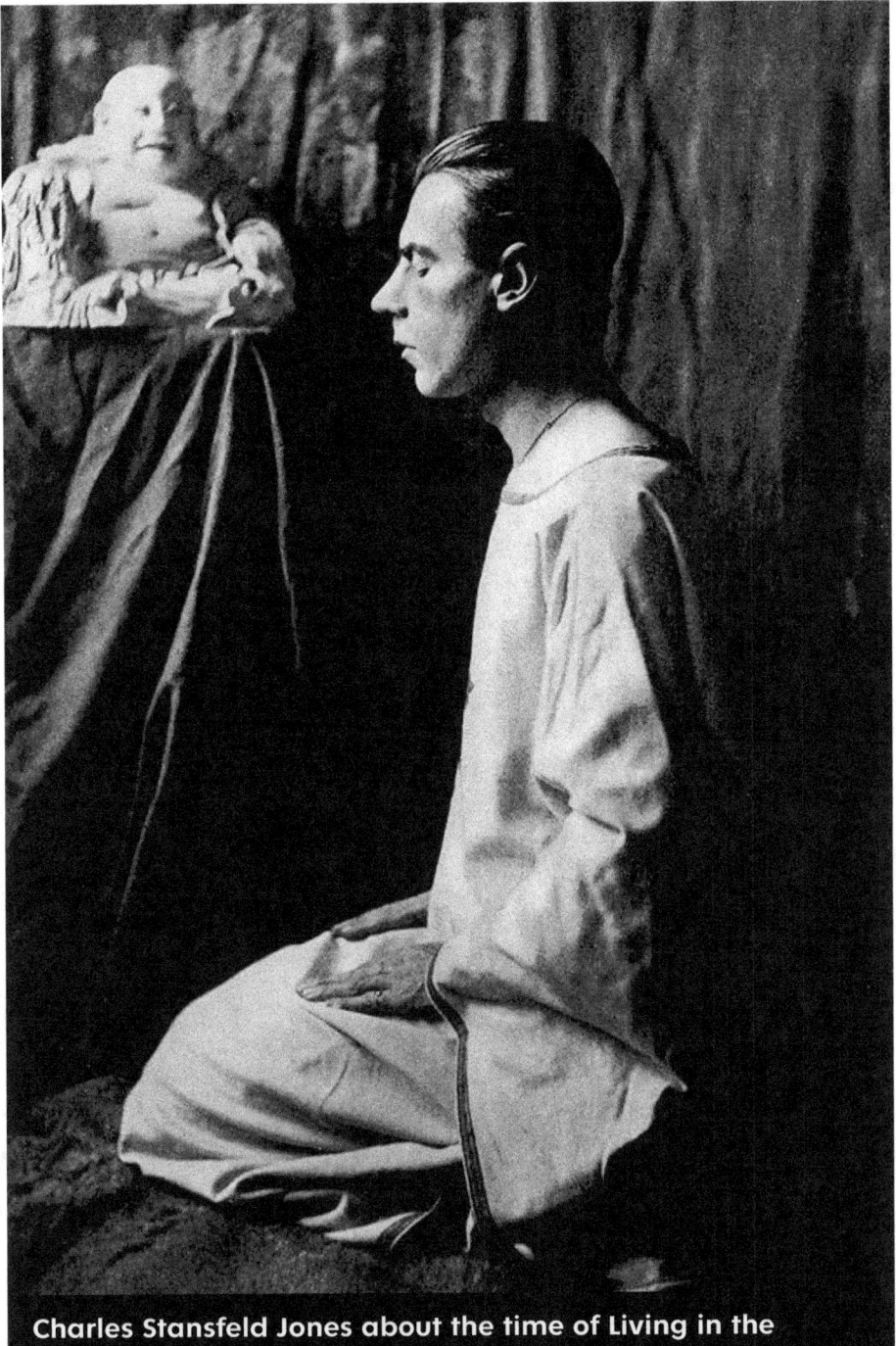

Charles Stansfeld Jones about the time of Living in the Sunlight. Portrait by Henry B. Camp, originally published in The Equinox III:1 (1919)

Chapter 5
Abodes of Evening

The second reference in the Living in the Sunlight letter which I cited in Chapter 2 is a brief "PS" or postscript note. It's an afterthought from Crowley. You have probably noticed by now that Crowley nowhere explains *how* to practice Living in the Sunlight. He was expecting Hilarion to tell Jones (and she does in the next Chapter). Whereas the first reference focused on the *effects* of Living in the Sunlight, the second looks at *evaluation*. What is the "measure of success"?

Crowley says Living in the Sunlight "involves making everybody in your sphere reflect your radiance" and "If you have anybody about you miserable, it shows that your light is failing to penetrate." Our light or radiance should have a tangible and penetrating effect on the people around us. That is, there is a transfer of positive energy that can relight or recharge another's latent positive thought forms. (A miserable person, for example, has given too much energy to negative thought forms and thereby weakened their positives). And if you are really radiating within - if you have energized positive thought forms - you should be able to validate (radiate) that without. Remember that James Clear quote: "Relationships compound. People reflect your behavior back to you." For Crowley, "anybody" *means* anybody. He states that this criteria applies to anyone "miserable" around you - in your private life, your OTO life ("lodge") and even "casual strangers."

It might cause some consternation that Crowley's measure of success is so exacting. It is that black and white there's no room to move. You cannot blame anyone, anything, make excuses or attribute failings to any outside factor, condition or mitigating circumstance. It's all on you. While this degree of 'radiance' might seem like a tall if not impossible order, we might consider that the emotions of blame, humiliation, anxiety etc that look to external factors as causes of our shortcomings, are associated with the lower energies or levels of Consciousness (shame, guilt, fear etc). These are surrendered in the transfiguration to Courage. So if you are really Living in the Sunlight, it actually is all on you! Through observation and self assessment we can discover more about the effect we are having and how we can influence the moods and behaviors of those around us.

Such an uncompromising "measure of success" demands the self-honesty to acknowledge your own inner defects or faults in character and practice. This can be done matter of factly and benignly, without beating ourselves up or re-energizing the Ego through self deprecation. Note Crowley's matter of fact admission: "I've not been a very striking success in the past." We can take heart from that, get over it and get on with it.

And I admit this is hard. That hard in fact it is difficult not to think that Crowley was over exaggerating an ideal to emphasize his point. Let's face it, we've all experienced (or know) that misery aunt who kills the mood every time they are in the room. Their persistent gloom, bad trip, and deep seated inner anger and resentment - their vampirism - drains everyone. Realistically, it might well be that it is not so much about "making everybody *in* your sphere reflect your radiance" (italics mine) as it is the radiating powers of attraction and repulsion *for* your sphere. "This also is compassion: an end to the sickness of earth. A rooting-out of the weeds: a watering of the flowers." *Liber XC:26*

A good indicator of how you are measuring up is your own level or state of happiness. Happiness is an inner psychological reward, it originates from within. Misery on other hand comes from the externalization of perceived sources of happiness, an overvaluation of those sources and the projection of that value, creating attachment and the desire for acquisition. This is a throwback to our base animal survival instincts - the getting of things from *out there*, eg. food, shelter, territory, a mate. In the yogic and tantric maps of the subtle body, we attribute these qualities to the lower 3 *chakras*.

There can be a tendency for energy or Mind to get stuck or stagnate in these lower animal centers. In such situations, emotions commonly dominate or replace logic and reason, leading to obsessive mentalisation (opining, rationalization, reprocessing, evaluating, judging). To radiate and penetrate your Light to others, you have to empower and inspire. Ultimately, that is done by rejecting your own egocentricity and by spiritual devotion which flows into our energetic system as enthusiasm or lovingness. Such non-linear, self-effulgent, radiance shines light on misery - other names for which, if we are to call a spade a spade, are vanity and narcissism. For if "a man's foes *shall be* they of his own household" (Matthew 10:36), then "Ye are the light of the world. A city that is set on an hill cannot be hid. Neither do men light a candle, and put it under a bushel, but on a candlestick; and it giveth light unto all that are in the house." Matthew 5:14-15.

We can come to a deeper understanding of radiance by considering what it is not. Here we must spare a thought for the miserable in light of Crowleyan psychoanalysis, which seeks a root cause in sexual desire. In *Liber Aleph*, a book that I've previously mentioned, Crowley devotes a number of analects to the management of disciples. Beginning with analect 96 ("On Directing Disciples"), he explains how the various distempers in students are usually the result of "the Desire of Sex unsatisfied." He counsels "shewing them the right Importance of Love, how it should be a sacred Rite, exalted above Personality, and a Fire to enlighten and serve Man, not to devour him." Next, in analect 97 ("On Certain Diseases of Disciples") he says "since Love is the Formula of Life, we are under Bond to assimilate (in the End) that which we fear or hate." In analect 98 ("On Watching for faults in the House") he gives final caution, "And beware most of this Love, because it lieth so close to Will that Dis-ease thereof easily imparteth his Error to the whole Way of the Magician."

"O ye that drink of the brine of your desire, ye are nigh to madness! Your torture increaseth as ye drink, yet still ye drink. Come up through the creeks to the fresh water; I shall be waiting for you with my kisses."

– *Liber LXV IV:6*

While it is tempting to think Crowley is reading too much into it all (does it always have to come down to sex?), consider that throughout this book so far, Sun, Self, Phallic Consciousness, kundalini, libido, kingly power, sexual force and magical force have all been closely associated. It is clear that living in these (or rather, living in *this*) is the Key to energic radiance. If that sounds a little out there or too freaky for you, consider how mild-mannered Napoleon Hill's tenth step in *Think and Grow Rich* was "The mystery of sex transmutation." There's something in all of this! Something energic. And if it is a secret, *it is an open secret.*

The paradox in aligning and equating these 'different' aspects of Self is resolved in Jung's idea of the *psychoid* - something that is both psychic (Spirit) and physical (Matter) in nature, *these being reflective of each other.* Like Jungian archetypes, this also gives the psychoid an *objective reality.* As Jung mentioned in the Introduction, the Sun is the fructifier and creator of all that lives, the source of energy in our world. "Our life substance, as an energic process is entirely Sun."

One expression of this solar-Phallic energy is in the sexual nature of an individual. In the interplay with Life experience and that postmodern abdication of personal and social integrity we call moral relativism, this can get corrupted, confused, abused, clouded, distorted, denied, misled, misused, misguided, mistaken, repressed, suppressed or oppressed. A lot of the world's misery is right there! Desire is one of the downward spiral levels of Consciousness and energy. It is below that beginning of Virtue we have called Courage. It is non life-affirming and leads to craving, disappointment and enslavement. Admittedly, there is also constructive desire where through the exercise of will, choice and decision we can elevate our level of Consciousness. Here though, and especially in terms of the sexual nature, we are concerned with frustrated or distorted wantingness - again, a throwback to our evolutionary origins and the need for external sources of energy to satisfy drives. These got linked to survival (and fear), and over millennia morphed into those desires and wants we find sublimated or elaborated in our social settings and expressions. They can lead to obsessive, risky and a host of other psychosexual and pathological behaviors. Remember that desire was one of the "elements" that Crowley stated had to be eliminated in the first Living in the Sunlight reference.

Ironically, it is quite probable that at least some of Crowley's views on student struggles with drive and desire were actually about Hilarion. The record shows that over the course of her affair with Crowley and their sex magical operations, Hilarion at times internally struggled with the moral, spiritual and physical considerations of the act. Who hasn't lived in that glass house? The ideal being set in this Chapter might seem impossible. It pays to remember that we're human. You need to be realistic and honest.

In this second reference, Crowley also makes some light hearted remarks about influence and persuasion that (lest you think otherwise) are more Carnegie than Macchiavelli. Notwithstanding my comments above on thought forms, I'd take these with a grain of salt, as alluded to earlier. Despite his optimism in the letter, Crowley rarely had a "romp through life." He is however, in part, referring to the politics and power plays of lodge life and leadership in a fraternal organization (OTO). Given that running lodges does not infrequently get described as analogous to herding cats, if Living in the Sunlight makes lodge life a little easier to manage then more power to it! Take Crowley seriously, just not *too* seriously.

To summarise this Chapter:

When you're smilin', when you're smilin'
The whole world smiles with you
When you're laughin', when you're laughin'
The sun comes shinin' through...

Chapter 6
The Starry Abode

"There is light within a person of light, and he gives light to the whole world. If he does not give light, he is darkness."
— *Gospel of Thomas*, Logion 24

By now we have a good idea of the types of results we can expect from Living in the Sunlight, as well as our measure of success. By introducing a map of Consciousness and the Way of transfiguration and surrender - by affirming Self over Ego - we have already inferred in general terms what the Living in the Sunlight practice entails. It is time to get to the practical steps to make a start.

Crowley's student Charles Stansfeld Jones became a published author and spiritual teacher in his own right, most commonly going by the name Frater Achad. Like Crowley, he too courted controversy (if less colorfully) and attracted both criticism and ridicule. Ironically, most of it came from Crowley himself after their relationship soured from the early-mid 1920s. That attitude has carried over blindly and uncritically to at least some of Crowley's modern followers. If you fall into this category, as I've said earlier in regards to knee jerks about Crowley, I'd consider the emotional pay-off or energy that holding on to that position provides?

We lack a critical examination and review of Frater Achad, which is a little surprising as he was a prolific author, lecturer and man of letters, devoting most of his life to instructing students through a number of different organizations. One thing that gets missed in Crowley circles about Achad is that he reflected a wider and uniquely North American spirit of his times. There is some merit in looking at him through that lens.

It was what the philosopher and psychologist William James called "the religion of healthy-mindedness" that was "passing over our American world."

Amidst this unusual religious fervour in the late 19th and early 20th Century North America, Achad was right in there amongst it all alongside spiritual healers of all varieties, spiritualists, transcendentalists, mesmerists, freethinkers, free-love advocates, black liberationists, Freemasons, Christian socialists, Christian scientists, occultists, New Thought, Theosophists, sex magicians, American tantrics, and many others. What could such a mixed bag possibly all have in common? They all picked up on one simple and quintessentially American idea - the use of mental force or mind power to create change and achieve outcomes. The early decades of the 20th Century in the USA marked the beginnings of what we might now call the positive thinking movement. From humble and at times quite bizarre origins, that shared mindset has gone on to influence numerous self-help groups, business motivational programs, tv evangelism, motivational psychology, therapeutic spirituality, as well as the New Age, wellness and other movements.

This new American phenomenon lacked Old World esoteric elitism, secrecy and snobbery. With New World optimism and egalitarianism, it spread across social stratifications through town hall meetings, barnyard preaching, soap box sermons, lecture circuits and mail order correspondence courses. The historian Mitch Horowitz called it the "ever-present, every-man-and-woman wisdom of our time" when "metaphysics morphed into mass belief." For Horowitz, this "is the backstory of modern America." Without it, for example, there would be no Oprah, no Dr. Phil and no Tony Robbins. No winning friends and influencing people. No thinking and growing rich.

Achad put himself out there as a lecturer and author, adding Thelema to the metaphysical melting pot. He spoke and wrote in everyday language, in stark contrast to Crowley's refined, learned, bookish and often complex and cryptic, eloquence. For Achad, Thelema was *the* "every-man-and-woman wisdom" and "religion of healthy-mindedness" for the times. As fascinating as all of this might be to consider, here we are concerned with two points only. First, the evidence clearly shows that some of Achad's lecture material came directly from Crowley, or was influenced by his times and training with Crowley. Second, *one of the lectures in question was titled Living in the Sunlight.*

The Living in the Sunlight lecture was delivered on 7 May 1922. This is nearly seven years after the Crowley letter to Jones about Living in the Sunlight that we have looked at. So for Achad at least, it is fair to say the practice was still front of mind. Thankfully, a transcript of the lecture survived and was published in the Swedish research journal, *The Fenris Wolf* number 7 (2014). I will provide a brief overview and analysis below.

Achad begins by identifying a connection between Living in the Sunlight and living with Thelema. He sees Thelema's *The Book of the Law* as the Way to "a life of pure joy under the law of Light, Life, Love and Liberty" and "our chance of immortality." This "life of pure joy" is life in the Sunlight. The sentiment is similar to what we have already read (or deduced) from Crowley. Achad goes a little further to describe and account for those he sees as living without the Sunlight, or in the shadows and darkness. Otherwise, Achad basically preaches Crowley's Magical Doctrine, that "true aspiration of growth" requires becoming conscious of "our true will, our true purpose." The "secret" for Achad (and this is pure Crowley talking), is "aligning...with the will of the Universe or God" and then "showing forth the powers of God by means of that will." We could substitute "Universe or God" with Tao or Sun.

After continuing to espouse Thelema, Achad then takes to some biblical exegesis, interpreting Matthew 8:20 - "And Jesus saith unto him, The foxes have holes, and the birds of the air have nests; but the Son of man hath not where to lay his head" - as a reference to Christ as the eternal Sun. "The sun itself, is always shining. It does not die and is re-born. It is constantly ever-living, and that is the idea concealed beneath Christ's words. He is always shining. He is always the Son of Man." (Achad continues this line of thinking in another lecture, "Christ & the message of The Master Therion," the latter being Crowley's name as the prophet and Magus of Thelema).

Achad goes on to make some references to the solar teachings of OTO. That is nothing new to what we've already seen alluded to or covered. Achad is more specific and technical (too technical for here), citing how the occult formulae of Tetragrammaton and Pentagrammaton relate to OTO teachings. Achad then identifies *what is living* in the Sunlight as *"Prana*, the life force." Again, there's nothing new for us there either. It equates with the energic. He identifies *prana* in relation to the formulae mentioned before as a "secret of the Holy Spirit."

Prana is then used to segue into a discussion about Kundalini, and the important OTO doctrine (and practice) that "the solar force or the Kundalini force... [should be] in the solar plexus and not at the base of the spine. This is its normal home to which we must restore it." After a discussion about certain mystical powers this enables in the Initiate-practitioner, Achad concludes that "these powers are to be obtained thru the living furnished (?) of the sunlight, every one of us" (the lecture transcript has some obvious errors).

Achad then mentions Crowley and Hilarion. Of import to us is that he mentions Hilarion's Living in the Sunlight practice and gives a commentary.

Achad recalls:

"When we were in Vancouver, some years ago, a certain sister of the Order whom we called [Soror Hilarion] came to visit us with the Master Therion [Aleister Crowley]...She it was who first used the expression "living in the sun light" and who has most successfully shown it forth in her own life."

Describing Hilarion as "one of the most wonderfully bright, cheerful, soothing individuals and yet at the same time full of passion," he tells us "she had a method all her own *which everyone one of us may adopt.*" (emphasis mine).

The method then follows:

"It consisted in this: she said that whatever may have been the cares and trials and troubles of the day, no matter how many people may have gone against us and appeared to be unkind to us and so on - no matter what the state of mind we have been in - there was one great secret. This world, itself, is more or less an illusion and we create to a large extent our own illusions. As a matter of fact, when I say the world is an illusion, I will say that we are looking at it from an illusory point of view. Now, the idea was that every morning - every night, when she laid down to sleep, she put aside the cares of the day - all little annoyances and sorrow and shadow, with a firm determination, before sleeping, to wake up with the sun and to wake up to a new day - to a clean sheet, to look at the world afresh every morning and live that day in the sun light and with the sun."

It's as simple as that. Achad explains: "practically everything we see, at one time, is sorrow and at another time is pleasure. It is a question of our viewpoint. If we begin to learn to take the point of view of the ever-shining sun, we shall find that all around us is light and beauty...If we become one with the sun, we should no longer see his rays as coming and falling on us, but we should see them as we project them on to our surroundings; then wherever we throw them will be sunlight, for we, ourselves, will have become the sun and the giver of light."

Achad faithfully observes Crowley's measure of success: "Now the test of [...]'s this: if we aspire to live thus, we must do all that we possibly can to refine ourselves, to cast out all that is dirty or unclean in ourselves or in our surroundings - to live royally as we are, as a representative of the sun upon earth, and not to be content that we are truly living in the sunlight or giving out the sunlight while there is any trace of darkness or distress anywhere in our surroundings...If we shall have succeeded in doing that, we shall succeed in not only living in the sun light - we shall have succeeded in becoming one with the sun and look at all things from the solar point of view."

Achad concludes by again praising Thelema and *The Book of the Law*, noting "when we have succeeded in radiating the true sun within us, which is after all the true Christ Spirit, when we can say "I and my Father are One" [John 10:30] - that my father is in Heaven and that Heaven is within me - then we shall realize what Christ meant when he talked about the Son of God, for each of us is a Sun of God, and we should all have that sun giving out the strength and light and [...]."

He ends by saying "I hope some of you will try to adopt some of these simple methods. You will find your relationships with all around you taking on a more pleasant feeling, and will find joys of which I have no possible opportunity to talk to you today...we shall begin to live naturally and freely as children of God and his representatives in the Kingdom." Amen.

Chapter 7
The Stainless Abode

Hilarion's practice was described by Achad as:

"Now, the idea was that every morning - every night, when she laid down to sleep, she put aside the cares of the day - all little annoyances and sorrow and shadow, with a firm determination, before sleeping, to wake up with the sun and to wake up to a new day - to a clean sheet, to look at the world afresh every morning and live that day in the sun light and with the sun."

We can break this up into four simple steps.

First of all remember that Hilarion's "great secret" was the realization that "This world, itself, is more or less an illusion and we create to a large extent our own illusions." What does she mean by that?

Hilarion is acknowledging the illusory point of view of the Ego. Understanding this is one of life's greatest Secrets. It is the life-changing inner realization and awakening that is the lamp to your own feet on the spiritual path. The counter to this illusion is to identify with what we have been referring to as the psychoid or energic Sun - that is, the physical energic Sun of our solar system and the spiritual psychological Self: to know and experience these as One and the same. Or as Jung said in Chapter 1, to see our life substance as "entirely Sun." To that point and point of view, we've already looked at Consciousness as energy, and the Sun as "the source of energy in our world."

The result of that identification, says Achad, is that "we, ourselves, will have become the sun and the giver of light." "If we become one with the sun, we should no longer see his rays as coming and falling on us, but we should see them as we project them on to our surroundings; then wherever we throw them will be sunlight." This projecting or throwing is what Crowley refers to as "making everybody in your sphere reflect your radiance."

You could call this transfiguration a shift in perspective, point of view, or an upgraded version of reality. Once you've made that initial shift, you are constantly upgrading to newer versions, relative to your level of Consciousness. Those levels or hierarchies become the frameworks of spiritual systems. In our Sunlight system, each time we reach some new level we transcend egoic illusion and "cast out all that is dirty or unclean in ourselves or in our surroundings - to live royally as we are, as a representative of the sun upon earth."
"We shall have succeeded in becoming one with the sun and look at all things from the solar point of view." "We shall begin to live naturally and freely as children of God and his representatives in the Kingdom." "You will find your relationships with all around you taking on a more pleasant feeling, and will find joys of which I have no possible opportunity to talk to you today."

Nor do I. It has to be experienced.

Step 1.

It is important here to note that I am reformulating the words of Hilarion, Crowley and Achad into a workable method. Every instruction from them about Living in the Sunlight has been faithfully published in this book. I am now translating that into a practice you could work with, *personalise and develop*.

Note the comment by Achad, "every morning - every night, when she laid down to sleep..." *Do this practice just before falling asleep.*

There is now an abundance of science (and pseudo-science) on the function of sleep. The states of sleeping and dreaming also figure in the analytical psychology of Jung, and in psychophysical, contemplative traditions such as the nocturnal yogas found in Tibetan Buddhism. The spiritual teacher Andrew Holecek, who wrote a brilliant book on Tibetan dream yoga, told Tricycle magazine in 2018, "I encourage people to consider the nocturnal practices; 95 percent of our so-called conscious life is dictated by unconscious processes. Until we bring those unconscious processes to life, which is what we do in dream yoga, they will run our life. By engaging in these practices, we can really work with profound transformation."

What I will cautiously say here without making any tall claims that have not been (and perhaps can't be) scientifically proven, is that the winding down brain waves associated with the pre-sleep period, those relaxed and suggestive states of Alpha or even Theta-frequency associated with the neocortex slowing down, are conducive to auto-suggestive programming and execution by the autonomic psychophysical (nervous) system, during sleep. *Living in the Sunlight is meant to work autonomously.*

Steps 2 and 3.

At this pre-sleep time, "...she put aside the cares of the day - all little annoyances and sorrow and shadow, with a *firm determination*, before sleeping...". (emphasis mine). *Reflect on the pain points of the day, your thoughts and feelings, and surrender them (let go of them) to Self.*

If you had a day that couldn't have been any better, lucky you! Surrender yourself anyway, to the Sun-Self and your highest spiritual intention. Let go of the Ego. The good days or the bad days of earth, for our purposes, are an illusion.

It is critical you do this with "firm determination."
You have to mean it. There must be intent or will. I would add to that *elevated emotion*. Fall in love with the practice, the Self and the Sun. It needs to be taken seriously and practiced in a spirit of acceptance, devotion, gratitude and surrender.

Step 4

For the first few minutes when you wake up you're in a similar brainwave pattern to what you were in just before you went to sleep. At this time, with the same intention and elevated emotion, resolve to *"look at the world afresh every morning and live that day in the sun light and with the sun."*

(I recommend revisiting the synopsis of Achad's lecture given in the last Chapter in light of this and the Appendix, Achad's "Stepping Out of the Old Aeon and Into the New").

That is basically it. Pretty simple, right? Consistency and determination is Key. As Crowley would teach, *Inflame thyself in praying*. A tell-tale sign of progress is a notable change in attitude or perspective, greater inner conviction, calmer, more positive and resilient days, a joyous mood, more energy, a more tolerant demeanor and as the "putting aside" practice gets better, improved sleep. The effect is cumulative. This book was designed to open up your Awareness to maximize the effect. *What you come up with to say or pray is up to you.*

It will take a certain discipline. Let's face it, before falling asleep you are sleepy, and when you first wake up you are drowsy. Students can find it hard to regularly maintain a practice:

"Weary, weary! saith the scribe, who shall lead me to the sight of the Rapture of my master? The body is weary and the soul is sore weary and sleep weighs down their eyelids; yet ever abides the sure consciousness of ecstacy, unknown, yet known in that its being is certain. O Lord, be my helper, and bring me to the bliss of the Beloved!" *Liber LXV IV:28-29*

What I have called discipline above is really an Awareness of the Unconscious tendencies or qualities of the phenomenal universe behind (in our case) these sleeping, waking and transitory states - not to resist them, but to 'go with the flow'. In Hinduism, the underlying tendencies to these states are called the *Gunas* - *Rajas* (activity), *Sattva* (lucidity) and *Tamas* (obscurity). When blind to them, the *Bhagavad Gita* describes the *gunas* as binding the Spirit within the body. With Awareness (energized attention) which is That which is beyond them, the *Gita* declares you will partake of the Amrita, the dew of *eternal life*. Put another way, to consciously utilize radiation involves and includes a creative tension and interplay with conduction and convection.

Keep in mind that Achad's account is from a motivational public lecture and not an instructional class. His description of Hilarion's practice must be subjected to experiential observation and analysis. Perhaps the most important delineation this bears out is that *thoughts are engendered by the emotions.*

Emotions are far more raw, basic and primitive than mental processes. They sit closer to the Unconscious. So, to "put aside the cares of the day," to put aside the "trials and troubles of the day," to put aside "how many people may have gone against us and appeared to be unkind to us," to put aside your "state of mind," to put aside "all little annoyances and sorrow and shadow," means *letting go of and surrendering the emotions behind your thoughts.* Address the feelings first and foremost, and their by-products go with them.

How do we know to let go of the emotions through surrender to Sun-Self? This may come across as gender stereotyping in these non-binary times, but let's not forget that Hilarion was a woman. *Living in the Sunlight is a woman's practice.* It factors in the 'feminine' right-brain function of intuition. Intuition is commonly connected with emotionality, sensitivity, and is considered more dominant in women than men. Intuition includes the capacity to read and feel the vibrational energies and thought forms of our emotional interactions. These affect your state of mind and this is what you are letting go of. Hilarion is talking about emotional (intuitive) release, not just (conscious) cessation of thought forms. Without acknowledging and releasing the emotions, you are more likely just suppressing or repressing their accumulated pressure (thoughts). That is not Living in the Sunlight. That is to live "every morning and live that day" in a pre-conditioned future based on an imprinted past. Another name for that self-imposed slavery is Living in the Nightmare!

Negative feelings impair body organs. You may remember earlier I quoted Crowley on "the magical Force in Man, which is the sexual Force applied to the Brain, Heart, and other Organs, and redeemeth him," and I wrote about how there is tendency for energy or Mind to get stuck or stagnate in the lower 'animal' centers (*chakras*). Unrelinquished emotions can affect the endocrine and nervous system as imbalances or enter the autonomic nervous system. That is a recipe for illness. On the other hand, by Living in the Sunlight, by releasing the emotions with intent into the Unconscious, the Self will automatically arrange for positive energy to flow back into your life. This is the innate drive to Wholeness. To let go of illusory and dispersive emotions and thoughts is to be left in the present, the presence of the inner Life of Self, invulnerable and invincible.

Sol Invictus is thy name!

One last point, keep in mind that by its very nature you might not realize Living in the Sunlight is working for you. Think about it - if you fully surrender something it has disappeared from Consciousness. So how can you be conscious of it? You may not realize how far you've come along and what you've gained. This is why charting activity in something like a journal can be a surprisingly useful aide. So can taking up the practice with a group of friends so you can debrief, observe each other over time, and swap notes and practice tips. This point highlights why Living in the Sunlight can be so powerful, effective and efficient while "doing nothing" (kind of).

Its apparatus is more Unconscious motion than conscious action. It is Tao. That "which achieveth all Things by doing nothing." Before you know it, Living in the Sunlight will be second nature. You'll barely be conscious you're even doing it.

Chapter 8
Living in the Sunlight

"It means merely sunlight. You may call me Little Sunshine."
-Aleister Crowley in court, questioned on his identification with the number 666

While the poetry of Living in the Sunlight is pretty easy to appreciate - the dark clouds of self are removed and the Sun of Self shines forth - I'll end by trying to shed some light on exactly *what* it is that is shining. This phenomena represents the transpersonal power of the energy field, not of the individual. As the dark clouds are removed, this energy and our ability to not only only accept it but project or radiate it outward, increases progressively.

We have seen this in the expression of Compassion and Love. Another name for the Love I am referring to is a state of Oneness. In the Western mind in particular, what passes as love is passing emotionality and little more than a neurosis covering interior conditions of dependency, attachment and possessiveness. The energy field on the other hand emanates from Self (remembering our Jung, the source of all energy is "entirely Sun") and is best described as *spiritual energy*. When we look at the levels of Consciousness we've been using, the influx of this energy commences with the 'upward' energy of Courage and progressively increases. All of the levels we have described are really just One in progression, or *Light in Extension*. Yet we get there in the nocturnal darkness of the Unconscious. As emotional pressure is released from the body, it has effects on subtle physiology (eg. the *chakras*), behavioral kinesiology (eg. the meridian channels) and brain physiology (eg. a shift from predominance of the left-brain to the spiritually oriented right brain). We start noticing this in ourselves as we let go of narcissistic and egoic self-interests and gains for forms of selflessness, service, Compassion, devotion and dedication. At the mystical level, this type of nonlinear inclusiveness leads to transcendence, illumination and revelation. The inner subjective experience of innate existence is no longer anchored in the presumption that the personal self (with a small 's') is the causal and effective agent. Such a recognition - the beginnings of Awareness of the true state of Reality - is the path towards Enlightenment. Living in the Sunlight keeps you mindful of and participatory in this journey, day after day.

I want to stress that a night-time practice has tremendous potential, not least of all for cultivating lucidity and using it to transform your waking life, to explore the presence of emptiness and deep states of reality and Truth, and to better relate to suffering, happiness and Compassion. Working through the night, like the Sun, you are always shining, you are always On. Rising and setting are but the perceptions of earth - the world of sleep or death. You are now, remember, "in the sun light and with the sun." *You are heliocentric not geocentric.*

As J. Daniel Gunther commented in *Initiation in the Aeon of the Child*, "The geocentric perspective alone considers the sun as "rising" or "setting" and the earth as the fixed point. The sun shines just as brightly on the far side of the planet at midnight. Sunset is only an "event" on the earth; from the point of view of the sun there would be no such perception."

And the rest, my friends, is up to you. I wish you godspeed.

"Let not the failure and the pain turn aside the worshippers. The foundations of the pyramid were hewn in the living rock ere sunset; did the king weep at dawn that the crown of the pyramid was yet unquarried in the distant land?"
— ***Liber LXV*:V:51**

"I am internally thrilled with constant joy."
– Aleister Crowley, letter to David Curwen (1945)

Appendix
Stepping Out of the Old Æon and Into the New

Frater Achad (Charles Stansfield Jones)

Originally published in *The Equinox* III:1 (1919)

Do what thou wilt shall be the whole of the Law.

As all of you should know, we have entered a New Aeon. A Higher Truth has been given to the World. This truth is waiting in readiness for all those who will consciously accept it, but it has to be realized before it is understood, and day by day those who have accepted this Law, and are trying to live it, realize more and more of its Beauty and Perfection.

The new teaching appears strange at first; and the mind is unable to grasp more than a fragment of what it really means. Only when we are living the Law can that fragment expand into the infinite conception of the whole.

I want you to share with me one little fragment of this great Truth which has been made clear to me this Sun-Day morning: I want you to come with me - if you will - just across the border-line of the Old Aeon and gaze for a moment at the New. Then, if the aspect pleases you, you will stay, or, it may be, you will return for a while, but the road once opened and the Path plain, you will always be able to get there again, in the twinkling of an eye, just by readjusting your Inner sight to the Truth.

You know how deeply we have always been impressed ith the ideas of Sun-rise and Sun-set, and how our ancient brethren, seeing the Sun disappear at night and rise again in the morning, based their religious ideas in this one conception of a Dying and Re-arisen God. This is the central idea of the religion of the Old Aeon, but we have left it behind us because although it seemed to be based on Nature (and Nature's symbols are always true), yet we have outgrown this idea which is only apparently true in Nature. Since this great Ritual of Sacrifice and Death was conceived and perpetuated, we, through the observation of our men of science, have come to know that it is not the Sun which rises and sets, but the earth on which we live which revolves so that its shadow cuts us off from the sunlight during what we call night. The Sun does not die, as the ancients thought; it is always shining, always radiating Light and Life. Stop for a moment and get a clear conception of this Sun, how He is shining in the early morning, shining at mid-day, shining in the evening, and shining at night. Have you got this idea clearly in your minds? *You have stepped out of the Old Aeon and into the New.*

Now let us consider what has happened. In order to get this mental picture of the ever shining Sun, what did you do? You identified yourself with the Sun. You stepped out of the consciousness of this planet; and for a moment you had to consider yourself as a Solar Being. Then why step back again? You may have done so involuntarily, because the Light was so great that it seemed as Darkness. But do it again, this time more fully, and let us consider what the changes in our concept of the Universe will be.

The moment we identify ourselves with the Sun, we realized that we have become the source of Light, that we too are now shining gloriously, but we also realize that the Sunlight is no longer for us, for we can no longer see the Sun, any more than in our little old aeon consciousness we could see ourselves. All around us is perpetual Night, but it is the Starlight and the Body of Our Lady Nuit, in which we live and move and have our being. Then, from this height we look back upon the little planet Earth, of which we, a moment ago, were part, and think of ourselves as shedding our Light upon all those individuals we have called our brothers and sisters, the slaves that serve. But we do not stop there. Imagine the Sun concentrating His rays for a moment on one tiny spot, the Earth. What happens? It is burnt up, it is consumed, it disappears. But in our Solar Consciousness is Truth, and though we glance for a moment at the little sphere we have left behind us, and it is no more, yet there is *"that which remains."* What remains? What has happened? We realize that "every man and every woman is a star." We gaze around at our wider heritage, we gaze at the Body of Our Lady Nuit. We are not in darkness; we are much nearer to Her now. What (from the little planet) looked like specks of light, are now blazing like other great Suns, and these are truly our brothers and sisters, whose essential and Starry nature we had never before seen and realized. These are the 'remains' of those we thought we had left behind.

There is plenty of room here, each one travels in His true Path, all is joy.

Now, if you want to step back into the Old Aeon, do so. But try and bear in mind that those around you are in reality Suns and Stars, not little shivering slaves. If you are not willing to be a King yourself, still recognize that they have a right to Kingship, even as you have, whenever you wish to accept it. And the moment you desire to do so you have only to remember this - *Look at things from the point of view of the Sun.*

Love is the law, love under will.

Works Cited

Abrahamsson ed., Carl. *The Fenris Wolf 7* (Edda, 2014)

Brady, Joel. *Baphomet*. Unpublished mss.

Churton, Tobias. *Aleister Crowley in America: Art, Espionage and Sex Magick in the New World* (Inner Traditions, 2017)

Clear, James. *Atomic Habits: an easy & proven way to build good habits & break bad ones* (Penguin/Random House, 2018).

Crowley, Aleister. *777 and other Qabalistic Writings* (Weiser, 1982)

Crowley, Aleister. *Commentaries on the Holy Books and Other Papers (The Equinox IV:1)* (Weiser, 1996)

Crowley, Aleister. *The Golden Rose*. Unpublished tss. OTO Archives.

Crowley, Aleister. *The Law is for All: the authorised popular Commentary to The Book of the Law* (New falcon Publications, 1996)

Crowley, Aleister. Liber Aleph vel CXI *The Book of Wisdom or Folly* (93 Publishing, 1991)

Crowley, Aleister. *Tao Te Ching (The Equinox III:8)* (Weiser, 1995)

Crowley, Aleister. *The Vision and the Voice with Commentary and other papers (The Equinox IV:2)* (Weiser, 1998)

Gunther, J. Daniel. *Initiation in the Aeon of the Child: The Inward Journey* (Ibis Books, 2009)

Gunther, J. Daniel. *The Angel & The Abyss* (Ibis Books, 2014)

Hill, Napoleon. *Think and Grow Rich* (Vermillion, 2019)

Holecek, Andrew. *Dream Yoga: Illuminating your life through lucid dreaming and the Tibetan yogas of sleep* (Sounds True, 2016)

Horowitz, Mitch. *Occult America: White House Séances, Ouija Circles, Masons and the Secret Mystic History of our Nation* (Bantom Book, 2009)

Horowitz, Mitch. *One simple idea: how positive thinking reshaped modern life* (Crown, 2014)

Jones, Charles Stansfeld. "Christ and the Message of the Master Therion" https://www.100thmonkeypress.com/biblio/achad/downloads/christ_and_the_message.pdf

Jung, Carl. *Psychology of the Unconscious* (Dover Publications, 2003)

Krauze, Lauren, "*How far are you willing to go to wake up?*" https://tricycle.org/trikedaily/far-willing-go-wake

Liber X *Porta Lucis*
https://lib.oto-usa.org/libri/liber0010.html

Liber XXX *Librae*
https://lib.oto-usa.org/libri/liber0030.html

Liber XC *Tzaddi vel Hamus Hermeticus*
https://lib.oto-usa.org/libri/liber0090.html

Liber LXV *Cordis Cincti Serpente*
https://lib.oto-usa.org/libri/liber0065.html

Liber CCXX *AL vel Legis, The Book of the Law*
https://lib.oto-usa.org/libri/liber0220.html

Londraville, Richard & Janis. *Dear Yeats, Dear Pound, Dear Ford: Jeanne Robert Foster and her Circle of Friends* (Syracuse University Press: Syracuse, 2001)

Pine (trans.), Red. *Lao Tzu's Taoteching*
(Copper Canyon Press, 2009)

Notes

Notes

Notes

Also available from IN PERPETUITY PRESS

THE LEGEND OF ALEISTER CROWLEY

https://thelegendofaleistercrowley.com

Currently available from In Perpetuity Publishing.

For more information about our publications please visit https://www.otoaustralia.org.au/publications

Available through all good online booksellers.

This facsimile edition of P. R. Stephensen's 1930 broadside against the 'Campaign of Personal Vilification Unparalleled in Literary History' arrives in 2021 as the mainstream media thrashes in its death throes.

Quality digital scans of the original book, never before published material from the Australian OTO archives, as well as a new essay examining the politics of conspiracy and the pathologies of Fake News, make this an indispensable case study of media malfeasance and moral panic.

Also available from IN PERPETUITY PRESS

THE BEST OF OZ

https://thebestofoz.com

After 13 years and 50 Issues, OTO Grand Lodge of Australia is making its member-only OZ magazine available to the public in this 'best of' compilation. Inspiring and provocative, OZ chronicles the birth and early development of the Australian Grand Lodge experiment in thought leadership, scholarship, culture and magical design.

ISBN 978-0646815770

Origins of the modern O.T.O in Australia ◊ Aurora Australis: topological reflections on the modern M.M.M. in Australia ◊ 'New Commentary' Theology: Notes towards reorganising the EGC Part 1 & Part 2 ◊ 'From the GM' (AUGL in Japan) ◊ Toiling in the (local) fields of Our Lord ◊ Remembering Parsi Krumm-Heller (1925-2008 e.v.) Obituary ◊ Grand Master Shiva's Introduction to J. Daniel Gunther's 'Initiation in the Aeon of the Child: the Path of the Great Return' ◊ Veni Cooper-Mathieson ◊ Woman Girt with a Sword ◊ EGC Retreat Keynote Address ◊ Our Church – the Clarity of Vocation ◊ Shadow of the Thelemites: the Abbot, the Abbey and the Nightmare ◊ In the Flesh – Manifesting Liber 194 ◊ Battle of the Ants ◊ Apokalypsis 418 – The Temple of Christ, the Angelic priesthood and the Great Return of the Queen of Heaven ◊ Temple Mount: The Oriental Templar crusade for Verità ◊ Living In The Sunlight

Also available from IN PERPETUITY PRESS

ORA ET LABORA

https://ora-et-labora.site

With wide-ranging and highly eclectic essays from around the world, Ora Et Labora gathers together the research and findings of the practitioner-scholars of Thelema.

ISBN 978-0645103908 Vol I
In the Weaves of the Order ◊ Typology of Will in writings of Aleister Crowley, Meister Eckhart and Carl Gustav Jung ◊ An Analysis of Liber Librae ◊ When meditation goes bad ◊ Health in Thelema: The Stone of the Wise & The Holy Guardian Angel ◊ Eros daimon mediator and Electoral College ◊ On the Epiclesis ◊ Secret Light: Reflections on the Rosy Cross ◊ Eucharist: From Self to God ◊ The Proof is in the Pudding ◊ Baphomet

ISBN 978-0645103915 Vol II
Āmi Satya: Hallaj, Crowley, and the Baul Fakirs of Bengal ◊ Carl Kellner ◊ Freemasonry, the OTO, and Crowley ◊ Aleister Crowley: a K2 Letter ◊ The Spiritual Heritage from Egypt ◊ Notes towards a preliminary analysis of a peculiar motif in the Stele of Ankh-af-nakhonsu ◊ The Birth of the New Aeon: Magick And Mysticism of Thelema from the Perspective of Postmodern A/Theology ◊ Crowley, Conspiracy, Moral Panic and the Media ◊ The Will of the Aeon

ISBN 978-0645103922 Vol III
Alba ad Rubrum: Waratah Blossoms ◊ Lord of Life & Joy ◊ The 'Occult Macrohistory' of Aleister Crowley ◊ Mundus Imaginalis, the Stone of the Wise ◊ Bread and Salt: To be taken with a grain of salt ◊ Initiation and the Hermetic Tradition ◊ The mantras and the spells: Language and magick ◊ "Anything can be Animated": The Visionary Cinema of Jordan Belson and its Esoteric Core ◊ Occultists, Nazis, Atlanteans and Alawites Vril and the Occult Revival ◊ 'That I may follow and dispel the night': Wagner's Parsifal and Liber XV ◊ A Crack in Everything : Finitude and the Ceremony of the Introit ◊ Temple Theology in the Gnostic Mass · Apokalypsis II: Temple mysticism in the New Aeon : An Introduction ◊ The Island of Flames and the spiritual heart ◊ Excursus on Notes towards a preliminary analysis of a particular motif in the Stele of Ankh-af-na-khonsu

ORDO TEMPLI ORIENTIS
Grand Lodge of Australia

SYDNEY ◊ MELBOURNE ◊ BRISBANE ◊ CANBERRA
HOBART ◊ PERTH ◊ ADELAIDE

www.otoaustralia.org.au

ORDO TEMPLI ORIENTIS
International Contact
www.oto.org

www.ingramcontent.com/pod-product-compliance
Lightning Source LLC
Chambersburg PA
CBHW072020290426
44109CB00018B/2294